TABLE OF CONTENTS

CHAPTER I	:	Prologue
CHAPTER II	:	Introduction
CHAPTER III	:	Ecommerce
CHAPTER IV	:	Selling Digital Products
CHAPTER V	:	Content Creation
CHAPTER VI	:	Freelancing
CHAPTER VII	:	Micro tasks and gigs
CHAPTER VIII	:	Professional services
CHAPTER IX	:	Investment Opportunities
CHAPTER X	:	Summary
CHAPTER XI	:	Legal Considerations
CHAPTER XII	:	Conclusion

PROLOGUE

Welcome to **"TOP 35 PROVEN METHODS ON HOW TO MAKE MONEY ONLINE"** your comprehensive guide on how to navigate the vast and dynamic world of online income opportunities. If you are here, it might be because you came across all the different, confusing information on the internet, of everyone claiming that they made thousands or even millions from doing several things online.

Since covid years, the number of people making money from online platforms has drastically increased, businesses make profits of more than 50% through online advertisements and the number of influencers has also shot up high. Who can blame them? I, too, wouldn't want to miss the opportunity of having an online passive income.

This has led to a lot of contradicting information on the internet, people trying to teach others how to make money, always through selling courses or something. I accumulated a lot of trashy information from the thousands of articles on the internet, the instagram gurus selling courses, tiktok guys asking you to join websites through their links and not forgetting the youtubers.

It was all so confusing and I wasted months trying to figure out what works for me while purchasing courses and memberships, which mostly did not work. At some point, I believed that I was the problem and kept on asking myself , "Why is everyone around me making six figures from online opportunities while I am not even seeing a possibility of me earning a penny?"

I then had a realization of how many people get misled or frustrated because of the not so straight information, not forgetting to mention those that start and give up shortly afterwards due to picking niches that don't suit them.
The most important thing that people tend to ignore is that making money online is a business and not a hobby, it's not something that you just consider doing in your free time. It should be treated in the same seriousness, time, focus and energy that is put into starting a business.

There are several factors to consider before choosing the type of niche that suits you. Keep in mind, what worked for your friend, might not work for you. And that is totally fine. After all, Hey! I am writing about 35 proven ways to make money online, there has to be something for you.

Lastly, most people mistake this as a get rich quick kind of scheme. You will get an earning equivalent to the work you put in, of course except for the lucky ones who just get famous in a blink and get gigs right away.

INTRODUCTION

The journey through this book is structured to guide you progressively from the understanding of the different 35 ways that are involved in making money online, their fundamentals and the art of mastering the strategies involved.

Whether you are a complete beginner or have a slight experience in the online world, this book suits you as it is designed to cover all important levels, ensuring that you can find the right strategies to fit your personality, needs and goals. Each section focuses on a specific method while providing you with a step by step guide.

There are 7 (or more) different categories on how to make money online. This includes :

- Ecommerce
- Selling Digital products
- Content Creation
- Freelancing
- Micro tasks and gigs
- Professional services
- Investment Opportunities

ECOMMERCE

I am sure you have come across so many videos about ecommerce on the internet, especially the ones on drop shipping or affiliate marketing. E-Commerce is a profitable source of making money online if done correctly, it requires effort and strategy. You an make money through ecommerce by :

1. DROPSHIPPING

In simple terms, dropshipping is partnering with suppliers(i.e from Ali baba or AliExpress), who fulfill orders directly to your customers.This happens when you list products on your ecommerce store (i.e Shopify) and market them. You hold no inventory of these products. When a customer places an order, the supplier directly ships the product and you keep a portion of the sale price as profit.

Steps on how to get into drop shipping are:

- Find a winning product, it could be fashion, gadgets, baby products, home decor or accessories.

- Set up an ecommerce store. You can set up one on shopify and use the free user account.

- Find a supplier for your product i.e from Ali baba, Ali express or Auto DS.

- Run organic ads on instagram or tiktok. You can also run paid ads. Organic advertising is a long term marketing strategy as you are building awareness about your brand on the internet through free tactics like SEO, social media marketing, email marketing, blog posts. For it to be successful, create interesting content that adds value to your audience and encourages them to engage.

Although this type of ecommerce has more profits or a get rich quick type of feeling, you will constantly have to be chasing for the next hot product. Your key focus has to be on the evergreen marketing, by selling things that solve people's immediate problems or insecurities. (i.e household products, fitness and gym resources or baby products)

Sales marketing is a core factor in dropshipping. It is crucial to use seo keywords to gain traffic to your store. You can also consider paying for advertisements in order to gain a lot of traffic to your ecommerce store.

Choosing a niche that you are interested in or know more about will help you find the right words to describe the products that you are marketing, which then leads to more sales. People are more likely to buy stuff when they read a personal story attached to it knowing that you share a similar need. With better advertising strategies and a better looking store ,you will definitely win.

Your supplier plays a huge part in your business. If the products are from China, it's most likely useless. Sorry to say

this, but your dropshipping model will fail due to the outrageous poor quality, disastrous shipping time and bad customer service. You are likely to incur a loss due to the number of returns that you might get from your customer orders. Most of the suppliers from China have a difficult return policy.
 To avoid this, it's best to find reliable suppliers or if you insist on ordering from the china products, buy what you are marketing beforehand and test it to check its quality.

This is a work from home business, not a work from home job, you have to be on your toes at any given chance. It is not for the lazy. 9 out of 10 of drop shipping stores close after 4 months due to its needing and competitive nature.

2. AFFILIATE MARKETING

This is simply promoting a product that entitles you to getting a commission whenever someone buys through your affiliate link. You have to be sales driven and have a social media account that you are active on, it's okay if you do not want to show your face on social media, there are faceless digital accounts, I will get into that in a different section.

Steps on how to get into affiliate marketing :

- Choose a niche that you are passionate about and that is also profitable. Picking a niche that you are passionate about helps you create genuine content easily hence upscaling your marketing skills. The top 3 niches are **W**ealth, (talk about digital products i.e. courses about money, courses about how to do something, people are always looking for ways to have more money) **H**ealth and **R**elationships. Just make sure to be a little more specific. Pick products that have helped you in one way or another. If you have not used it, it's okay, just share experiences on how important that product is.

- Find affiliate programs and sign up to get approved to market their products, it could be physical products, courses, subscriptions or softwares. More than 86% of companies have affiliate programs i.e Amazon, Nike, Adidas, Sephora, Clothing brands, Household brands, so many.

- Create a social media account on i.e Instagram, facebook, tiktok, pinterest, youtube or google blogs, basically any online platform that you prefer.

- Start creating content about the product and market it. As I earlier said, you need to be sales driven. We are lucky to have AI in this digital age where we can use chat GPT to help us create trending content.

Another way that you can try affiliate marketing is by signing up on affiliate networks like **Clickbank.com , CJ Affiliate and Shareasale.**

Then look for the easiest, trending hottest topics to promote. That could be a travel niche. Go to the affiliate network website and type in travel, find something that you are comfortable with i.e tripadvisor, a company that will pay you a certain amount of money per click on the traffic (number of people) that you bring to their website.

Next, open a social media account and create content about travel. You can repost from other trending travel videos that you come across on the internet, add a link to your profile or preferably on the post. When people click on your link, that takes them to the trip advisor page, you are entitled to a certain amount of payment. Easy right?

The trick is in finding content that will get alot of views, use chat gpt to give you trending keywords that you can use in your posts.

Lastly, investing in a course is something that you can consider, it will help to know what you are doing on a deeper level, which then leads to figuring out the tricks faster and guides you on how to maneuver the digital space easier.

Count it as an investment.

The main problem is to figure out the real coaches and mentors. I would advise you to buy a 1:1 (one on one) course, rather than an ebook because there are some details that you can't simply understand just by reading.

 Clickbank.com offers free affiliate courses. Go to clickbank.com, click on affiliate on their menu options, and choose getting started on clickbank.

3. PRINT ON DEMAND

Print on demand is when you custom design products like tshirts, mugs, pillowcases or phone cases and sell them.You can start this without any capital or prior investment. Am sure you have come across print on demand products especially during the festive seasons like christmas, easter, new year, halloween , valentines day or others.

How to start an online print on demand business

- Create a print on demand account i.e on Printify, printful , gelato , e.t.c . This is the print on demand business that will help you create, print and ship your products to your customers when they place an order.

- Create a storefront or website, this could be done on shopify or etsy. Your storefront has to be appealing to the eyes, if not then you will get zero sales. Research on different websites to see what others are doing.

  On this storefront, you will design a theme that makes it appealing to the eyes, list your products on it and add prices .When fixing your prices make sure to consider the profit margin.Once you get an order from your storefront, the order will automatically be sent to your print on demand account, get manufactured and then shipped directly to your customers . Of course you will need to integrate the two accounts first (that is your storefront and print on demand platform). Shopify has guidelines on how to do that.

They have great customer service , and are always ready to help and teach you.

- Create your product. Pick products that you like and align to what you want to build into your business storefront. Make sure to research what people actually buy and not just what you find interesting.Go to canva and design whatever type of picture or information that you want to print on your products.

- Order a sample. Since you are not manufacturing but just creating the design, it's crucial to order a sample before selling. It's low cost, you can use printify as it has cheaper manufacturing costs. Use the free package when starting, although you are can earn more profits with premium.

4. AMAZON FBA (Fulfillment by Amazon)

Amazon FBA is a bit more complex as it requires you to invest money upfront. It involves you sending your products to Amazon fulfillment centers, where they handle storage, packaging, and shipping procedures when orders are placed. If your products are eligible for Amazon Prime and other benefits, your sales are more likely to increase.
You need a game plan that has to be followed strictly and done strategically. Most people refer to Amazon FBA as a high risk road.

You can start Amazon FBA using the following steps;

- Research and choose a niche. You need to conduct product research to find winning products. It's advised to use a software tool like **Jungle Scout, Helium 10, FBA or GROWTH UNI TOOL** that will help you to analyze market trends, sales data and competition.

- Find a product that meets your preferred niche and has good profit margins. While selecting a product, remember to have the size, weight and complexity into consideration as they affect shipping and storage costs.

- Source for products and reliable suppliers. It is crucial to first order samples from different suppliers to ensure quality. You can find suppliers on platforms like Ali baba, Global sources or local manufacturers.

This is the kind of business that you should not go on guessing about unless you want to lose your money.

- Calculate costs and margins. These include product cost, shipping fees, amazon fees, software purchase price and taxes. Ensure your selling price enables a healthy profit margin.

- Create an Amazon seller account. You can choose a selling plan between an individual or professional account. With an individual account, you pay a fee per item sold while with a professional one, payment is on a monthly subscription. You then list your products with high quality images and compelling descriptions using relevant keywords. Product photography is important, if you advertise your products with low quality images, you are preparing to fail.

- Ship your products to amazon fulfillment centers directly from your suppliers.

- Launch and advertise your products. To increase visibility, you can consider having promotions or giveaways to boost sales.

- Use tools like Amazon inventory management system to keep track of your inventory levels to avoid overstocking or stockouts.

- Lastly, provide excellent customer service by responding promptly to customer inquiries or issues. Maintain high ratings by ensuring timely delivery and product quality. Optimize your listing and monitor performance based on the customer data, advertising performance and sales data.

A trick before purchasing your inventory, is to list it on amazon first and see if it gets any notice before ordering to avoid having dead stock.

5. SELLING HANDMADE CRAFT

Starting an online craft business takes time and effort, it requires dedication and creativity to make it a profitable venture. I have seen people turn their hobby into an income. And that is always the best, as they do it out of passion. You can make handmade jewelry, candles, art, decor, knitted blankets or gift hampers.

- Identifying your niche is the first step, as it is in any kind of business. Think of the type of craft that you want to make or you already know how to make, be sure that it is on demand. Focus on creating unique products that are of high quality as it is crucial to maintain repeat customers.

- Set up an online store. I would recommend setting up stores in different platforms i.e Etsy, Amazon Handmade, Ebay, Golmagine, Marketplace by the Micheals, Artisans.cop or social media platforms like facebook, tiktok, instagram and pinterest.

- Your store needs to be appealing to the public eye. For this, take good high quality pictures. Ensure product pictures are clear and well lit, showcase multi angles as well.
- Write compelling descriptions of your products, talk about how passionate you are into creating your craft, add pictures of the

background while creating them as it builds a relationship with the people viewing your content.

- You can also mention the materials used and any unique features. Do not forget to add seo keywords to increase your chance of appearing on google.

- Price products appropriately. Research about similar products to determine the right price. Consider the cost of materials, time and effort put into it and desired profit margin.

- Marketing your products is also crucial, do so through ads or on your social media page. Plan for the shipping and packaging accordingly. The packaging is really important and it should be appealing. It should also be secure to avoid any kind of damage during shipping.

- Lastly, always provide excellent customer service. Respond to all inquiries almost immediately and professionally. Handle complaints with care to build a positive reputation.

6. BUYING AND SELLING USED ITEMS

This is a good way to make extra money. It takes a little more effort and time since you have to move from one place to another to source the used goods or sell them. You can also refurbish some of the goods before selling to increase your profit margin i.e old furniture

The step by step guide is in two steps :

HOW TO SOURCE FOR AND BUY THE USED PRODUCTS

- Choose trusted and reliable platforms like facebook marketplace, ebay, craigslist, offer up, etc. Use specific words to find what you are looking for. Look at the photos closely and read through the description in detailed form. Always look at the seller's ratings and reviews. Ask questions about the receipts, warranty or used period from the seller. Negotiate the price to secure a good deal. Use secure payment methods and pick public places to transact, bring a friend or family if possible.

HOW TO SELL THE USED PRODUCTS

- Choosing the right platform that suits the type of products that you want to sell. It could be Ebay, Facebook marketplace, Poshmark for clothing and

fashion items, Amazon that is suitable for books and other platforms.
- Take quality photos and write detailed descriptions of the item that you are selling. Include the brand, condition, size, color, and other relevant details. Set a reasonable price for the items considering its condition and always be willing to negotiate.
- Thereafter, create your listing on your prefered platform, use keywords that help your listing to appear on top of the search buttons.

SELLING DIGITAL PRODUCTS

If I am allowed to have favorites in here, then selling digital products would be the one. It allows me to work for myself by having my own business and being able to control everything. I get to create my own products, or purchase DFY Products (Done for You) , publish and market them on different websites, advertise the products on my social media faceless accounts and so much more. I guess it's a personal favorite since I love creating, managing and writing content. There are different ways you can participate in selling digital products including :

7. **CREATING AND SELLING EBOOKS**
8. **DEVELOPING ONLINE COURSES**
9. **CRAFTING i.e KIDS COLORING BOOKS, COMIC BOOKS**
10. **BUILDING JOURNALS AND TEMPLATES**

With the right products and correct marketing skills, digital products have an assured profit margin. The secret to making more money is by creating something that solves a problem. It could be you talking about things to do on a baecation, girls or boys trip, create an ebook on being pregnant or how to be a first mom, sell a course on how to create digital products, how to crochet or how to build things. Make kids coloring books or comic books. Meal plans or time table templates are always in demand. Create journals and add affirmations to it so as to add its value to the buyers. Once you brainstorm, you will find out that there are so many things to create.

Steps on how to sell digital products

- Find a niche. Write a list of 10 things that you are interested in, the audience that you relate to and ways that you can answer their daily questions. Out of the ten, research and find the most profitable and trending ones, that is what you should work on. It could be health and fitness, homeschooling, how to make money, anxiety and depression, the list is long. Use sites like wordstream and answerthepublic, to type in your niche keywords and confirm if it's a trending niche or not. Trending topics usually have a research number of around 30,000 and more.

- After selecting your niche, the audience that you aim to address, and finding workable solutions to the problems that they are facing. It's time to create your product. Canva is a great platform to design your ebook , as it has different templates that you can use for free if you do not want to pay for the subscription yet. Having an outline of how your digital product should look is important, you can always ask Chat gpt to write it down for you. If you are lazy and want chat gpt to write the whole ebook for you, then go back to the outline it gave you, and request for 500 words on each bullet point it mentioned. The con to this is, your book will miss a human touch and tone. It might sound vague. Although, you can always modify the content and give it an emotional feel. Transfer the content and create it in the design template that you chose on canva.

- Next is to choose a platform to sell your digital product. These marketplaces include Amazon kdp, Google play books, Apple books, Gumroad, Shopify, Etsy, Sellfy, Podia, Clickbank, Easy Digital Downloads, Fiverr and e.tc You can also sell them on your own website using wordpress or shopify. Create an attractive and user friendly online store. Ensure to include details such as product description, preview, high quality images and an easy checkout process.

- Determine the price of your digital product. The pricing should be based on factors like market research and competitor analysis. If you are just starting, consider offering discounts to attract more customers. Promote your products and utilize the paid advertising to reach a broader audience.

Selling digital products is advantageous as it does not require production costs or physical inventory. They can be sold in unlimited number of times without any additional production costs. Since the product is digital, you can reach customers worldwide without the limitations of shipping costs. This makes it possible to generate passive income as they continue to sell with minimal ongoing effort.

CONTENT CREATION

I guess that you already know what content creation is, even if it's not in depth, you do have a slight idea. Not just content creation but also influencers. Yes, the ones that you have a love and hate relationship with or the influencers that you stalk cause they entertain you and maybe also learn from.

Content creation is the process of generating ideas, producing, editing them and posting to your target audience. This content could be informational, entertaining, or educational. Content can be distributed in many forms, could be through blogs, videos, podcasts or social media posts. It's all about sharing knowledge, experiences and creativity to engage and build a relationship with an audience.

Prior to getting into content creation, you need to choose a niche in order to stand out. It should align with your passions, expertise and interests. Define your target audience by considering demographics such as age, gender, location and interests. Know how you can tailor your content to meet their needs and preferences.

To be successful in this, a strategic plan should be implemented. Develop a content calendar to schedule your posts and ensure constant delivery.

Create a content strategy that outlines your goals, target audience and the type of content you will produce. Define the key themes and topics that you will cover. Your strategy should be flexible to adapt to changing trends and audience feedback.

Through voice and style is how you communicate with your audience. It should be authentic and align with your brand values. It could be a friendly, humorous or informative tone. Your audience will always recognize your content through your voice and tone. The consistency in your tone will help in building a trusting and loyal following.

Tips and tricks on creating engaging content include :

- Knowing your audience. Tailor content according to your audience's interests, needs and preferences. You can use surveys, polls and feedback to understand what they want. Ensure your content provides value to keep the audience coming back, it could be educational, entertaining or inspirational.

- Use high quality images and videos. Most people are attracted to quality content, it builds credibility and loyalty. Focus on producing high quality content rather than frequent below bar posts. For written content, optimize for search engines with keywords and proper formatting. This increases visibility and attracts organic traffic.

- Implement storytelling techniques as this is a powerful way to connect with your audience. You can share your personal experiences and lessons learned.

- Authentic and personal stories build trust and relatability. Content that evokes emotions like surprise, joy or empathy tends to be more memorable and shareable.

Start earning money through content creation in the following ways :

11. INSTAGRAM…
12. FACEBOOK

Instagram and facebook have evolved beyond mere communication platforms. They are now powerful sources of passive income. Once you figure out how to monetize these accounts, you can make close to 6 figures, of course depending on your strategies, consistency and effort.

The steps needed to take this two platforms to leverage include :

- Understanding the platforms

    Instagram attracts mostly young people, as it is a visual centric platform that focuses mostly on photos and videos. Its features include reels, posts, stories and IGTV.

    Facebook on the other hand has a broader user base audience. It is good for B2C (Business to Consumer) and B2B (Business to Business) marketing. Its features include posts, stories, pages, groups and marketplace.

- Select a niche that you have passion in and are knowledgeable about. This is because you will need to constantly post about the selected niche. Examples could be Money and Wealth, Trading, Home and decor, Family and children, Food and nutrition, Pets, Health and Fitness, Travel, Mental Health and so much more.

- Build a strong profile. Choose a memorable and relevant username. You then need to add a profile picture that is professional but friendly, you can also decide to use a logo rather than a picture. A logo can easily be created on Canva. Write an interesting bio description that clearly states who you are and what you offer. Your bio has to be precise and use seo keywords to gain organic traffic. Add your contact information, not personal but professional because once your account blows up you will have so many people contacting you, and wouldn't want to get mixed up between the two. Make sure that the contact details are easily accessible. This could simply be an email address.

It is crucial to set your account as a business one rather than personal, have it set on creator mode. This is to enable you to have access to the analytics tools and know how your content is performing. With a creator account, facebook and instagram tends to boost the posted content to the people interested in your type of niche.

- Start creating engaging content by implementing these three different strategies:

  <u>Relatability</u>   with your audience to build connections.
  <u>Authority</u>   to show your expertise in your niche which builds trust.
  <u>Activation</u>   by encouraging your audience to take action and move to the next step.

  Focus on creating high quality content. Use stock videos if you are too busy to create your own. Consistency is important. Consider posting 2 reels, 6 stories and one post a day. Use trending audios that have been used in less than 2 Million reels and include 5 hashtags that are niche related in the posts and reels. This will help reach a broader audience.

  Prepare your content in advance to avoid burnout. Don't forget to include keywords.
  Have a mixture of different types of content, alternating within tutorials, how-tos, memes, behind the scenes, your products or services.

- Grow your audience. This can happen in two ways. Organic or Paid Growth.

  Organic Growth involves you engaging with your audience by responding to comments, sending and replying to direct messages, partnering with influencers in your niche either by commenting and liking their posts or participating in live streams and webinars with them . Research and use relevant hashtags to reach a broader audience.

Paid Growth involves boosting your high performing posts to reach a larger audience by promoting it. Use Instagram and Facebook ads to target specific demographics. Always monitor the performance of your ads using analytics tools. Adjust your target audience and ad spend based on performance data.

Note that I didn't mention buying an existing account or buying followers as this sometimes affects your account in the future.

- Monetize your accounts. I like Instagram and Facebook since there are so many ways that you can monetize them, including:

  Sponsored posts and brand collaborations. Once you have an audience built, brands tend to approach you with deals and partnership offers to promote their services. Negotiate your rates and their demands in a way that suits you and not make you feel pressured. Ensure to get paid in advance to avoid arguments and misunderstandings.

  Affiliate marketing. Promote products from other companies and earn a commission for each sale through your referral link. Showcase products that you have used or relate to in order to maintain trust with your audience.

Selling products and services. This could be physical products, digital products like ebooks or basically services that you offer. Set up a shop directly on the platforms or add links to your external storefront shops. To add several links, use websites like stan store, linktree and beacons. Some of the services that you can offer are consulting, coaching or freelance services.

Create a lead magnet in order to boost sales. This could be free products or big deal discounts. Always collect your followers' emails as this will be useful in future. With their email addresses, you can always send them newsletters about your products, talk about discounts and promotions or inform them when you are launching something new. Have an email marketing platform like flodesk or beacons.

13.   TIKTOK

Tiktok is the easiest platform to make money from compared to Instagram or Facebook. Through different surveys, it's proven that monetizing creators rely heavily on tiktok compared to instagram.

Tiktok is typically a social media platform that allows users to create, share and discover short form videos. It was launched by a Chinese company in 2016 and has over a billion active users worldwide.
The platform is algorithm driven and is tailored to showcase content according to your interests or needs on your FYP.(FYP - For You Page). This feature makes it easy for content to go viral.
Monetizing TikTok involves leveraging several income streams that the platform offers. These income streams include :

- **Tiktok Creator Fund.** This is a program that pays creators based on the views and engagement that their content generates. To be eligible you must be at least 18 years of age, have at least 10,000 followers and have accumulated over 100,000 views on your videos within the past 30 days. You can apply under the Creator Fund section through the app. The creator fund is not available in every country, although you don't have to worry as you can still earn from your videos by downloading your content from titok and posting them on youtube shots. Be careful to remove the watermark before posting on youtube shots. To learn more about monetizing on youtube after posting, check on the youtube section. If you don't want to post on youtube, do not cancel yourself too early as we have 5 more ways to have a passive income through Titok.

- **Brand Partnerships and sponsorships.** This form of monetization is highly profitable for Tiktok creators as companies are always in need of advertising their products and services. They are willing to pay creators to promote their business in videos. Once you have an audience built and strong engagement in your comments, companies tend to approach you. You can also find the partnerships through marketing platforms like direct outreach. Don't forget to negotiate your deals as some companies will just send you free products in exchange for a lot. Be careful. It's safer to receive a certain payment beforehand.

- **Live Gifting.** During live streams, viewers can send you virtual gifts that can be converted to real money. You need to be above 18 years and have 1000 followers to be eligible to go live. Gifting works when viewers purchase coins within the app. They then use these coins to buy gifts for the creator. When creators receive the gifts usually as diamonds, they can convert them into cash and withdraw through paypal or other supported methods. This form of monetization fully focuses on the goodwill of your audience.

- **Affiliate Marketing.** I know that I have spoken about affiliate marketing in almost all sections. This should make you look keenly into it. Just have a strategic approach that aligns to your brand as a creator. Include the affiliate links in your video descriptions and bio as well.

- **Selling products or services.** Leverage your account by selling merchandise such as clothing, fashion or digital products. You can create your products without any capital through print on demand platforms like printful and have them deliver it directly to your customer. These products can be sold on the tiktok marketplace.

- **Cross Promotion on other platforms.**
  To be more successful, diversify your income. Promote your content to other platforms like Youtube, Instagram and Twitch. Drive traffic on those platforms by encouraging your followers to follow or subscribe to your other platforms. On youtube you can earn through the ad revenue, instagram through sponsored posts and on twitch through subscriptions and donations.

Starting tiktok involves setting up an account by signing up, creating engaging content and building an audience. This can happen through the following steps:

- Determine a niche. It's so easy to go viral on tiktok. With all the different niches around, you can choose on anything and make it fun. I have seen people go viral by recording videos of them cleaning their homes, guiding other mums by sharing their experiences as new mums, showing off their hobbies or talents, people posting recipes and cooking videos, creating how to videos or get ready with me videos. Literally anything, don't overthink it. There are people who go viral by just sharing their life experiences with good storytelling techniques, hence entertaining their audience.Research on what other people are doing in the same niche as you and just start.

- Create an account. Choose a username that reflects your brand and personality. You can either add your logo or picture as your profile photo. Add a bio that describes who you are and what content you create. Make it short but interesting or funny. Link your other social media accounts to drive cross platform growth.

- Before creating your content, spend time on your FYP page to understand trending content in your niche and the popular hashtags that they use. Follow creators that you enjoy and find inspiration in their content. Start creating content, experiment with different video formats while incorporating popular sounds to increase visibility.

Remember that consistency is key, engage with your audience and optimize the algorithm by using relevant hashtags to make your content discoverable. Leverage the trends and challenges.
Analyze your video performance, audience demographics and engagement rates to help you refine your content strategy.

14.   YOUTUBE

There is a massive potential to earn revenue as a youtube streamer. Youtube offers numerous opportunities to generate income. It also provides a vast audience with over two billion logged in monthly users.Its diverse audience and robust monetization features can turn your passion into a profitable venture.

In order to be eligible to get paid on youtube, you need to either

- Have at least 1,000 subscribers and accumulate 4,000 valid public watch hours in the past 12 months.

or

- Have at least 1,000 subscribers and 10 Million public shots views in the last 90 days.

You also need to adhere to all Youtube's policies and guidelines. Once you are eligible, go to the youtube app and navigate to the monetization tab. Review and accept the youtube partner program terms. Sign up for Google AdSense and link it to your account. You will need to set your monetization preferences, including types and placements.

The different monetization methods include

- **Earnings from youtube views and ads.** You practically get paid from the number of views per advertisement connected to your video. You can have the advertisement at the beginning of your video, mid view of your video or on the right side of the video above the suggestion list. I have had people confess that the mid-view ads are amust as you earn more from it.

- **Brand deals and sponsorships.** Brands are always looking for influencers to promote their products. As your channel grows, you can always reach out to companies directly for the deals or join influencer marketing platforms like FameBit, AspireIQ or Grapevine Logic. When you get the brand deals, negotiate with them about timelines and having compensation upfront to avoid misunderstandings. You also need to be transparent with your audience by disclosing the paid promotions.

- **Affiliate marketing.** I have spoken about affiliate marketing in the previous chapters. You can sign up for affiliate programs to market products related to your niche. Include affiliate links in your video descriptions or pinned comments.

- **Channel memberships.** This feature is available to channels with over 30,000 subscribers. Consider offering channel memberships to your subscribers for a monthly fee. Members get access to exclusive badges, videos, live chats and more.

- **Youtube Premium Revenue**. All the youtube premium members pay a subscription fee to have ad free videos. As a creator, you earn a share of the fee based on how many premium members watch your content.

- **Merchandise shelf**. If you have over 10,0000 subscribers, you can use the merchandise shelf to showcase and sell your branded merchandise directly on your youtube channel. Integrate platforms like Printify to create and manage your products. You can refer to the section I talked about Print on demand to know more.

To get into Youtube you need to :

- Create a Google account that will give you access to youtube. Once you are on youtube, click on the profile picture in the top right corner and select 'Create a channel.' Follow the prompts to set up your channel name and details. Add a profile picture and banner that represent your brand. Complete by adding a description of what your channel offers. Use seo keywords.

- Before adding the description I hope that you already figured out what our niche is. It's crucial to know who your target audience is, their interest and the type of content they like. Do not overthink trying to identify your niche. Just take the first step and try something out, see what's trending and learn from your mistakes. Use tools like Google Trends and Youtube Analytics to gather insights.

- Create and upload videos. While starting, you don't need high end equipment. A good camera (which could be an iphone) and good lighting can significantly improve your video quality. As your channel grows, invest in better equipment. Enhance your videos with video editing software tools like Adobe Premiere Pro, Final Cut Pro and more. Remember to optimize video titles, descriptions and tags with relevant keywords to improve visibility.

- Plan your content in advance and be consistent in posting. Having a content calendar helps you to stay organized.

15. FACELESS DIGITAL MARKETING

Do you prefer staying anonymous but still earn an online passive income? Well, then faceless digital marketing is for you. Gone are the days where you needed to be a savvy influencer to make a mark on the digital space. With the revolution of faceless social media accounts, you can easily make your work and efforts profitable. Just have a keen eye for curating content that resonates with your target audience.

Faceless digital marketing refers to marketing strategies that do not rely on personal branding or the use of individual personalities to promote products, services or brands. Instead stock videos or photos are used to highlight the brand's story, values and benefits. This type of marketing highly depends on visual elements for the brand like logos, color themes, design and aesthetics. One of the hottest trends within this space is the creation of faceless short videos. These short, engaging video clips are not just entertaining and eye-catching but also money magnets. You can incorporate faceless digital marketing on platforms like instagram, facebook, tiktok, youtube, twitch and other social media platforms.

Some famous examples of faceless digital accounts include the social media football pages, meme pages, funny videos pages, celebrity gossip pages and so much more.

Steps of getting into faceless digital marketing are as follows :

- Pick a niche. A well chosen niche can be the difference between a thriving faceless account page and one that struggles to gain traction. Refer to the section under Selling digital products and follow its steps on how to select a proper working niche. After selecting your niche, dig deeper by assessing what the competitors in your niche are doing while incorporating faceless marketing skills.

- Set up your faceless digital marketing account on the social media platform that you prefer. It is highly recommended to practice cross platform promotion. This is where you post your content through your different social media accounts i.e Instagram, Tiktok, Youtube, Pinterest and Facebook to gain a broader audience. Add links of your different social media accounts to each one of them. Use a relevant and catchy username that defines your niche. Your bio and description should also be interesting. Use niche related keywords to improve discoverability.

- Content selection and consistency. Find content (photos and videos) that you can post on your pages. You can find stock content from websites like pixel, shutterstock, canva and others. If you are looking for appealing and aesthetic stock content you can check on platforms like my vanilla gallery, content cove, social stocks co and soulset club.
Consistency is basically the backbone of online success. Regular posting helps to keep your audience engaged and also boost your algorithm to gain organic

traffic. Always schedule your content to stay on track and avoid burnout. Use scheduling tools like Later or Buffer.

- Engage with your audience. Reply to their comments, private messages and even consider following them. Use 4 - 5 hashtags that are niche related. Engage with other creators in your niche too. Run occasional giveaways and discounts to boost engagement on your content.

- Monetize your page. There are different ways that you can monetize your page and account. Refer to the sections under Instagram, Tiktok and Youtube to know the ways to do it.

- Track and analyze your content to get insights needed to understand your audience, get a clear direction on how to produce your content and increase your earnings effectively. Pay close attention to metrics like Reach, Impressions and Engagement Rate. These will give you a good idea of how well your content is performing.

16.   BLOGGING

Despite the traditional assumptions that people have towards blogging. It still remains a powerful and versatile platform for making money online, regardless of all the rise of social media and video contents.

I am certain that when I mention writing a blog, most people think of the diary style that was popular in the past. Blogging is now more strategic and keyword focused. All the information, diagnosis, recipes and research that you look up on google are from blogs.

In order to have a successful blog, choose a niche that is trending and not super competitive. The reason why I would advise not to go for a competitive niche is due to the fact that google tends to favor people with credentials and professional certifications. Use tools like Google trends, Keyword Planner, and SEMrush to identify topics that have significant audience interest. Once you start blogging, understand who your readers are, what they are looking for and how your content can meet their needs, you can use google analytics for this as it helps you know what content performs and what doesn't. Invest in Rank IQ that helps you have a google strategy.

When you are certain of the content that really performs from your blog posts google analytics, make more twists and angles about that topic.

Set up your blog by :

- Choosing a blogging platform. Popular blogging platforms include WordPress.org (Its self hosted) , WordPress.com, Blogger and Wix. Having a self hosted platform instead of renting is often recommended because of its flexibility and control. Every successful blogger that I know uses wordpress.

- Choose a domain name. Select a memorable and relevant domain name that reflects your personality and your niche. Use domain registrars like GoDaddy or Namecheap to buy your domain.

- Sign up for a web hosting service. Hosting will provide the server space and resources needed for your blog to be accessible online. Some of the web hosting services are Bluehost, SiteGround or HostGator. I would highly recommend Bluehost. You then need to install your blogging platform i.e WordPress. Most web hosts offer one click WordPress installations, hence making it easy to set up your blog. Follow the prompts on your screen to complete your installation.

- Customize your blog. Go for a professional theme that suits your niche and set it up in a way that reflects your brand. Have an appealing theme and be extreme with the keyword research.

- Start creating high quality content. Have headlines that are attention grabbing and accurately reflect the content of your posts. You can use headline analyzers for this. Set up specific days that you will be posting in order to stay consistent and maintain regular posting. This helps build an audience and improve your blog's SEO.

You can get paid for blogging in the following ways :

- By integrating Ad Networks. **Google Adsense,** which is the most popular, displays ads on your blogs and pays you based on clicks or impressions. You can work with them through signing up for an AdSense account. **Media.net**, this is an alternative to google adsense. It's particularly effective for niches like finance and technology. **Direct ads,** is the highest paying form of ads. You get to sell your ad space directly to companies. To attract the companies, have an 'Advertise Here' page to attract potential customers.

- Join affiliate programs that go in harmony with your niche.

- Collaborate with brands and write about their products. This is also known as sponsored content .

17. PODCASTS

A podcast is a digital audio program consisting of audio episodes that are turned into series. It was called audio blogging in the past. The difference between youtubers and podcasters is that, youtubers have a video involved while podcasters it's just their voice. Lately, most podcasters are having video podcasts in order to reach a broader audience.

Before monetizing your podcasts, you need to have a solid foundation. These include high quality content creation, consistency and engagement with your audience through email newsletters, social media or feedback.

Setting up a podcast involves :

- Invest in high quality equipment for producing clear and professional audio.

- Choose a quiet space with minimal background noise with no echo or ambient noise.

- Use reliable recording and editing software i.e Audacity that is free, Adobe Audition and GarbageBand for Mac users.

- Have a brand name, Logo, Intro and Outro that state a brief description of your podcast.

Once your podcast setup is done, you need a hosting platform to distribute your episodes to various podcast directories. Select a reliable hosting service that will store your audio files and generate RSS feed for distribution. Some of the podcast hosting services include LIbsyn, Podbean or Anchor. The major podcast directories are Spotify, Apple podcasts, Stitcher and Google podcasts.

There are different ways that you can monetize your podcast. These include:

- Through sponsorships and advertisements.

- Listener donations are also effective, it relies on the goodwill of your listeners.

- Merchandise sales. This could be print on demand items like mugs, tshirts, stickers and more.

- Promoting affiliate products and earning a commission for each sale made.

18. CREATING STOCK PHOTOS AND VIDEOS

In today's age, content is everything, for businesses, personal needs and so much more. Marketors, businesses and content creators are in constant search for high quality stock footage to enhance their posts and projects without the need for additional filming. This has created an opportunity for photographers and videographers to monetize their skills by selling stock photos and videos.

Stock footage are pre shot images and footage available for licensing to people that need them. By uploading your content to stock agencies, you give permission to the buyers to use your footage hence providing you with a passive income source.

While there's a market for almost every type of stock footage. The most bought themes are
- Lifestyle: People engaging in daily activities, family moments and fitness
- Protests involving politics and war.
- Nature and wildlife
- City scapes an travel
- Business and technology: Office environments, professional headshots and tech gadgets.
- Abstract and backgrounds.

You can get started on creating and selling stock photos and videos by :

- Have equipment like a decent DSLR or mirrorless camera for photos and a camera with good capabilities that will enhance your work. Invest in editing software such as Adobe Lightroom for photos and Adobe Premiere Pro for videos to edit your content before uploading.
- Build a diverse portfolio and focus on themes to attract a broader audience. Ensure your work is well organized and versatile.
- Choose a platform to sell your photos and videos. You can choose to use **Stock agencies** like Shutterstock, Adobe Stock, iStock, Pond5 or Getty Images.
- When uploading content, ensure that it is high quality content. Your images and videos should be sharp, well composed and free of noise or artifacts. Keywords and descriptions are critical for discoverability. Although, be careful to avoid keyword stuffing as it can harm your visibility.

To increase your sales and marketing, try to stay current and updated to popular themes and seasonal trends. Use social media to market your work and drive traffic to your stock portfolio. Embrace your journey and stay creative, watch your efforts transform into a rewarding source of income.

19. PINTEREST

Pinterest is a search engine and not social media. It is more than just a digital pinboard for collecting fashion inspiration, recipes or decor ideas. With more than 450 million active users, it is a powerful platform for building awareness, driving traffic and generating income.

Pinterest is basically a visual search engine that offers users new ideas and inspirations through images and videos. You can set up your pinterest and have the potential to create revenue by:

- Creating a pinterest business account. This gives you access to the analytics and advertising tools. You will get to know which posts are doing well and who your audience is.

- Pinterest being a search engine, its search functionality is driven by keywords. It is crucial to conduct keyword research using the Pinterest Trend tools and search bar to discover what users are searching for. You should also do competitor research.

- Craft an eye catching profile. Your bio should be engaging and informative. Include your other social media links like instagram, facebook, tiktok and blogs to market them. Use search engine keywords everywhere to increase traffic.

- Since Pinterest works completely by visual attraction, high quality and eye-catching images or videos are essential. Vertical images in the ratio 2:3 perform the best. You can incorporate canva to design your images.

- Create valuable pins that are more likely to be saved. You can create how to guides, infographics, checklists and tutorials that cater to your audience's interest. Make sure to pin something 3 - 8 times everyday.

- Pinterest also highly relies on consistency. Consistency makes your brand more recognizable. As a beginner, you can post 5 - 20 times in a day. That's a lot I know. It's the reason why **Tailwind** exists. It helps you schedule your content and post right one time. Once you have your content scheduled with them, you can choose to rest and spend a day or two without being online and still have your content uploaded.

- I would advise one to get a course if you really want to get into pinterest at a fast rate.

Monetize your pinterest through:

- Affiliate marketing. Promote products that are relevant to your niche by creating pins that link to your affiliate products.

- Drive traffic to your blog or website. Create pins for each of your blogs or website posts with optimized pinterest search. This can lead to increased ad revenue, email subscribers and sales.

- Selling products. This could be clothes from print on demand or your handmade products, courses, ebooks and so much more.

- Having sponsored content once you have built a following.

FREELANCING

This is a flexible way of working, people tend to offer their skills and services to clients on a project basis, it is mostly on a contract. As a freelancer you can work independently, schedule things according to your own work preferences, set your own rates and choose the projects that you want to take on. Freelancers are considered to be individuals that pursue their passions and tend to achieve a better work life balance. Ways that you can make money online as a freelancer include

20. **Virtual Assistance**
21. **Graphic Design**
22. **Video Editing**
23. **Web Development**
24. **Voice over Work**

To do this, you need to create a portfolio showcasing your best work, the most famous platform is Linkedin.
You then need to choose a freelancing platform where clients seek freelancers. Some of the well known platforms include : **Upwork, Freelancer, Fiverr, Toptal and Guru.**

Create a professional and well detailed profile on those platforms mentioning your skills, experience and don't forget to include your portfolio because a well crafted profile attracts potential clients.

Bid on smaller projects when starting to gather positive reviews and a good reputation on your profile. Research on what your competitors are charging and set your rates accordingly. Do not overcharge or undercharge.

Focus on delivering high quality work as it will bring you repeat customers. They are likely to provide ratings. The star ratings will then influence you into getting higher paying projects.

Networking is crucial, join online groups or communities related to your field, you can find them on facebook or linkedin. This always leads to collaborations or job opportunities.

MICRO TASKS AND GIGS

Micro gigs and tasks are assignments that you complete online to get paid. They vary from different tasks and you can find them on different sites. These tasks include:

**25.	ONLINE SURVEYS**

These are the quickest and easiest to start, although they pay less. It is not something that will make you rich but it will give you extra pocket money. Literally anyone can do it .

You can make money doing surveys on applications like Attapol, Octopus, Eureka, Pure profile, Influence, Life points, Branded surveys, Google rewards. Always select well established apps to avoid scams.

They all pay differently, while joining it is advised to use known platforms to avoid scammers.

To increase your chances of receiving surveys and earning more, sign up on several platforms. You can also increase your earnings by exploring other earning opportunities by joining referral programs. When someone joins the surveys through your link or code, you get to earn a certain amount.

26.   TRANSCRIPTION SERVICES

Transcription is the listening to audios or video recordings and converting them into written text. This service is becoming a crucial part of many industries i.e media, entertainment to legal and medical fields. Some of the skills needed to provide this service are listening skills, fast and accurate typing (a little thank you to google auto correct), attention to detail and time management skills. I could group transcription services into

- General transcription : This basically covers a wide range of audio content like podcasts, interviews, lectures or meetings

- Legal transcription : This often requires specific training or certification. It entails transcribing to legal proceedings, depositions or other legal documents.

- Medical transcription : It entails transcribing medical reports, patient notes and other health care related documents. It requires specialized knowledge because of the medical terms involved.

Pricing varies based on complexity of the transcription and your experience. Mostly, you get paid per audio minute or hour, per word, per page or just a flat rate.

How to get into transcription services :

- Build or sharpen up your skills. It is essential for you to be good at typing fast and accurately too. Practice with different audio files to improve your speed and accuracy. You can select a niche according to your skills as they all pay differently.

- Set up a profile on different websites to find clients. You can choose to start with websites like Rev, TranscribeMe or GoTranscript that always have transcription jobs available. If you want to work as a freelancer and get paid more, you can bid on projects on websites like Upwork, Fiverr and Freelancer. Networking also comes at hand, by joining communities or groups on different platforms like linkedin and facebook increases the chances of collaborations or potential clients.

Through honoring your skills, setting up an efficient online workspace and delivering quality work, it is possible to build a successful transcription business.

27. TRANSLATION SERVICES

The demand for translation services is at its all time high as the internet is breaking down geographical barriers. Businesses, authors, websites and individuals now frequently need content translated into different languages. Some of the skills needed in translating are proficiency in the source and target language, cultural knowledge of both languages, strong writing skills, ability to research and understand specialized terminology accurately and attention to detail. Translation services can be categorized into several types :

- Literacy translation which is the translation of books, poems and other literary works from one language to another.

- Business translation through translating business documents, reports and marketing skills.

- Website localization is about adapting websites to different languages and cultural contexts.

- Legal translation being the translation of contracts, legal documents and court transcriptions.

- Medical translation involves translating medical records, pharmaceutical instructions and health related documents.

You can start offering translation services by :

- Building your skills. You have to ensure that you are proficient in both languages. Consider acquiring certifications such as ATA certification (American Translators Association) or other relevant credentials. Practice makes perfect, use various texts to build your proficiency and speed.

- Create a workspace that is free from distractions as translation needs attention to every single detail. You can then find translation work online. Agencies like TransPerfect, Lionbridge and Gengo hire translators. Websites like Upwork, Fiverr and Freelancer allow you to bid on translation projects. You can also join associations like TA or ProZ to network with potential clients and other translators. Do not hesitate to contact business, authors or websites that you think might need your service.

To build a successful online translation business make sure to deliver high quality work by always proofreading your work before submitting, follow the guidelines that you were given, use translation softwares to ensure efficiency and stay organized to keep track of deadlines and client requirements.

28. TESTING WEBSITES AND APPS

The success of websites and apps largely depends on its usability, functionality and user experience. This is basically the testing of websites and apps to evaluate its products, identify bugs, check usability issues and overall user experience.Companies are willing to pay for valuable feedback from real users to improve their digital products.

To perform this service you need have a stable internet connection, use tools like Jira, Bugzills or Trello to document and track bug issues (only if you want to get deep into it as a professional) and to use websites like UserTesting, Testbirds and Utest to find the testing gigs.

You might need to send screen recording reports for visual feedback, hence tools like Loom or OBS Studio come in hand to record your testing sessions.

Steps of getting into Website and Apps testing include :

- Sharpening your skills. While formal education is not necessary, taking courses in web development, software testing or web design could be beneficial. Practice your skills by testing different websites and apps on your own, it builds your skills and understanding of common issues.

- Once you have all the needed skills, it's time to look for the testing jobs. You can find website and app testing assignments on platforms like Usertesting, Testbirds, uTest and Userlystics. These platforms connect testers with companies seeking feedback. If you want to work as a freelancer and bid on projects, use Upwork, Freelancer and Fiverr. Always keep in mind to network on social media too.

INVEST OPPORTUNITIES

Online investments have become a significant base for achieving financial growth. Traditional barriers are broken down as the accessibility of the internet is now widespread and technology is advanced, making it possible for people from all different backgrounds to participate in financial markets. Online investments offer a variety of opportunities from stocks, crypto currencies, NFTs to real estate crowdfunding and so much more. This means that anyone with an internet connection and willingness to learn can take control of their financial future. I personally think that everyone should think of investing online now as the value of the stocks keep going up and it's an opportunity not to miss. Instead of having all your money in savings or fixed deposits accounts, which offer low returns, it's best to have a percentage of your savings in online investments to yield much higher profits. Note that I said a percentage, as these opportunities also come with their own set of risks, it's crucial to understand both, the potential rewards and the possible dangers before diving in.

To succeed in the online investment market, it is paramount to constantly educate yourself. The financial markets are always evolving with new opportunities and challenges.

By staying updated and informed on the market knowledge, you can easily adapt to changes and make better investment decisions. There are several resources that can provide you with valuable insights and updates on the latest trends and developments.
These include Financial news websites, investment forums, online courses and webinars. Subscribing to reputable financial newsletters and following investment experts on social media would come at hand.

Every investment has a degree of risk, and online investments are no exception. We all know that the potential of high return is often accompanied by a significant risk. This means that, as an investor, you have to be prepared for the possibility of losing your capital.

The key to be successful in this type of investment is through balancing the risks and the rewards, something that you will learn how to do through research, strategic planning and being disciplined. Risk management is a critical skill in investing. Diversify and spread your investments across different asset classes and sectors to reduce the impact of poor performance on a single investment. The different ways that you can get into investment include:

29.   STOCK MARKET

When you purchase a stock, it means that you have bought a small piece of ownership in a company. The stock market is a prominent avenue for online investments. It offers people the opportunity to buy and sell shares of publicly traded companies. The stock market can be operated through exchanges, such as the New York stock exchange (NYSE), where buyers and sellers come together to trade shares. The prices can fluctuate based on supply and demand, company performance and broader economic factors. There are two primary ways that investors profit from stocks

- Through capital gains, where you sell your stocks for more that you paid for
- Through dividends, which is a portion of profit from the company being distributed to the investors.

To start trading stocks, you need to

- Open an account with an online brokerage. On the platform you will be provided with the tools needed to buy and sell stocks, track your investments and access market research. These online brokerages include Robinhood, Fidelity, Charles Schwab, Ally Invest, TD Ameritrade and E*Trade. When selecting an online brokerage, consider factors like fees, available trading tools, ease of use, reputation and customer support.

- Decide whether you will go for short term or long term investments. It depends on your financial goals and risk tolerance.
  Long term investing is when you purchase stocks and hold on to them for an extended period, it could be years or decades. Long term investments are also known as buy and hold investing. It requires patience and focus on the fundamental performance of the companies that you are investing in.

  Short term investing involves buying or selling stocks over shorter time periods, ranging from hours, days or months. This strategy seeks to capitalize on market fluctuations and price movements. It is a type of investment that could be very profitable, although you need to have a solid understanding of market trends, technical analysis and willingness to take on higher risk.

- Analyze the stock market or company that you want to invest in. There are two main approaches to analyzing stocks, fundamental and technical analysis.

Technical Analysis focuses on statistical trends and patterns in stock prices. This approach uses charts and technical indicators to identify potential entry and exit points for trends. It is mostly used by short term traders to make decisions based on price movements.

Fundamental Analysis involves evaluating a company's financial health and value through examining factors such as earnings, revenue, management quality, growth prospects and industry conditions. Key financial statements to review include the balance sheet, income statement and cash flow statement. Important metrics to consider are return on equity (ROE) , earnings per share (EPS) and price to earning (P/E)

- Once you have invested, you need to find effective risk management strategies to help mitigate the risks and protect your investments. Examples of common risks are market risk due to overall market declines, company risk which is associated with a specific company's poor performance, liquidity risk where you are not able to buy or sell your investments quickly at a fair price and lastly interest rate risk which is caused by changes in interest rates that negatively affect the value of your investment.
Reduce risks by spreading your investments across different assets , keep track of your investments and

make adjustments as needed based on market conditions and your financial goals. The core advise would be to use stop-loss orders to automatically sell a stock if its price falls to a certain level, limiting potential loss.

30. CRYPTOCURRENCIES

These are digital or virtual currencies that use cryptography for security. Unlike the currencies issued by the governments, cryptocurrencies operate on decentralized networks based on blockchain technology. The first and most well known cryptocurrency was created in 2009 and is called **Bitcoin**. Since then, thousands of cryptocurrencies have emerged i.e ethereum, tether, litecoin and others.

Cryptocurrencies have gained popularity due to their potential for high returns and their role in fostering financial innovation. They offer several investment opportunities from buying and holding to trading on exchanges . However, this market is highly volatile and investors should always be prepared for price swings.

To invest in crypto currencies you need to :
- Create an account on an exchange platform. Some of the popular ones are Coinbase, Binance, Kraken and Bitfinex. These platforms allow you to buy,sell and trade a variety of digital assets. When choosing an exchange, consider factors such as security, fees, user interface and the range of available cryptocurrencies.

- Deposit funds into your account using a bank transfer, credit card, or other payments supported by the exchange. Find the trading section of the exchange , select the cryptocurrency that you want to buy and place an order. After purchasing cryptocurrencies, transfer them to a digital wallet for safekeeping. When you leave your assets on the exchange, they might be vulnerable to hacking or any other security risks.

Digital wallets come in various forms.
Hardware wallets offer the highest level of security by offering your private keys offline. These wallets include Trezor and Ledger.
Software wallets are applications that you install on your computer or smartphone. They include Exodus or Electrum.
Online wallets / web wallets can be accessed through a web browser and are normally hosted by third party providers.

31. REAL ESTATE CROWDFUNDING

This is an investment model that allows individuals to invest in real estate with lower capital requirements compared to the normal real estate investment. Real estate crowdfunding is the act of investing in real estate projects by pooling funds from multiple investors through online platforms. Some of the famous online platforms include Fundrise, RealtyMogul, CrowdStreet, PeerStreet and Roofstock.

There are two types of real estate crowdfunding :

- Equity Crowdfunding, you as an investor get to purchase shares of a property or a real estate project. This entitles you to a portion of the rental income generated by the property or profits from its sale. Equity investments offer higher returns but higher risks as well, the success of the investment is tied up to the performance of the property and the market.

- Debt Crowdfunding, is when you as an investor lends money to property owners or real estate developers in exchange for regular interest payments. These loans are always secured by the property giving an extra layer of security for the investors. Debt investments offer lower returns compared to equity investments but are much safer due to the fixed interest deposits and the collateral backing the loan.

When considering real estate crowdfunding investments, it is essential to conduct your own research to evaluate the potential returns and risks. Things to consider include the location, property type, developer track record, the financial projections and the exit strategy.

32.   BUYING AND SELLING NFTs
(Non Tangible Token)

NFTs represent a revolutionary concept in the digital world, allowing digital assets to be bought, sold and traded on blockchain platforms. These digital assets could be artwork, gaming, music, virtual real estate or other digital collectibles. NFTs are bought, sold on popular platforms like Open Sea, Rarible, Foundation and SuperRare. Ownership of the NFT can be transferred by sending it from one wallet to another, with the blockchain recording every transaction to ensure transparency and security.

When investing in NFTs, you need to be careful and conduct thorough research as the market is still new and volatile. Platforms like twitter, discord and other specialized NFT new sites tend to have valuable information.
It is also crucial to evaluate the creator of the digital asset. You can look into their previous works and reputation in the community.

PROFESSIONAL SERVICES

Offering professional services online has been made possible by the transformation of the internet. Professional services that were once strictly face to face are now accessible at the comfort of your home, as long as you have an internet connection. This has created a platform for experts to reach a global audience, create flexible work schedules and generate income. I can say this gained more fame and turned into a normal thing after Covid, when people had to learn how to work online. Children were even attending schools from home. By following the best practices and continuously refining your approach, you can build a successful online business.

33. ONLINE TUTORING

After the pandemic, online tutoring has seen a significant rise in demand as more parents and students seek flexible and personalized education options. Whether you are a teacher, subject matter expert or simply passionate about helping others learn, online tutoring offers an opportunity to share your knowledge and earn from it.
How to set up your online business :

- Identify your niche. Focus on subjects that you are knowledgeable about and enjoy teaching. This could be mathematics, science, language or test preparations (e.g SAT)

- Choose an online tutoring platform. You can pick a platform that provides a built in student base, handles all your administrative work and payments. Some of the famous platforms include Tutors, Wyzant or Tutor.com. You then need to create a professional profile that highlights your qualifications, experience and teaching styles. To attract more attention, add testimonials from people that you have tutored before.

- Research market rates and set competitive prices. Consider offering a free trial session to attract new students. This could be your lead magnet. You can earn anywhere from 15 USD to 80 USD, depending on your expertise and subject matter.

- To deliver the best practice you, use interactive tools like virtual whiteboards and screen sharing to make the sessions engaging. Always tailor your teaching methods to individual student needs and learning styles. Seek feedback from students and parents to know how to improve your services.

34. COACHING AND CONSULTING

Coaching and consulting are broad fields that have a wide range of services, like life coaching, health and wellness consulting.
Coaching focuses on personal developments and behavioral change, while consulting involves offering specialized knowledge and strategic advice to individuals or businesses.

There are several types of coaching and consulting :

- Life coaching, helps your clients achieve personal goals, improve relationships and enhance overall wellbeing.

- Health and wellness coaching, focuses on improving your clients physical and mental health through personalized plans and support.

- Career Coaching, guides individuals through career transitions, job searches and professional development.

- Business coaching, assists business owners and entrepreneurs to start and grow their businesses, improving management skills and achieving financial goals.

- Marketing consulting, helps businesses develop and implement effective marketing strategies.

- Financial consulting, provides advice on financial planning, investment strategies and wealth management.

Build an online coaching and consulting business by following the steps below:

- Identify your niche by clearly identifying your area of expertise and the specific problems that you can solve. Consider obtaining relevant certifications to enhance your credibility, although it's not always required. I have seen health and wellness coaches that just show their work, personal growth and testimonials making people choose to work with them, not because of their credentials but the results they see.

- Set up your work space. Use the right tools for the video conference calls i.e skype, google meet or zoom. Make use of Asana or Trello as the project management tools that will help with the management of client tasks. To manage clients data, utilize HubSpot or Salesforce as your CRM Software. Scheduling tools include Calendly or Acuity.

- Create a Professional website. You need to clearly mention your services, showcase your work and include testimonials. Use professional design to instill confidence in potential clients. If you can not create a website, utilize social media platforms like facebook, instagram, tiktok, pinterest and others.

- Set up your pricing rates. Decide whether you will charge hourly, per session or offer packages. Research market rates in your niche to set up competitive prices. For payment processing and invoicing, you can use paypal, stripe, payoneer or others.

- Market your services. In order to get clients, you need to market your services. You can create content and be active on social media to gain an audience.

Remember you can still do it faceless, refer to my content creation chapter.

Post regularly to address common client challenges and showcase your expertise. Share valuable content, engage with your audience and participate in groups. You can also choose to publish blogs. Ensure that you provide high quality content to attract organic traffic. Network by joining online groups and participate in webinars in your niche to connect with other professionals and potential clients.

35. LEGAL CONSULTING

Legal consulting involves providing expert legal advice and services online. This type of expertise is ideal for lawyers and legal experts looking to expand their practice.
In order to do it, ensure that you are licensed to practice law in your jurisdiction and comply with local regulations

regarding online legal services. Start online legal consulting by :

- Acquiring your license and identifying the local regulations about offering online legal services.

- Pick your area of expertise. This could be family law, business law, intellectual property or so much more.

- Develop a professional website to showcase your services, expertise and client testimonials. Market your website by using SEO keywords and social media to attract clients.

- Use secure communication tools and case management software to protect client confidentiality.

SUMMARY

ASSESS AND UPSCALE YOUR SKILLS

A strategic approach to understand and leverage your skills is crucial if you want to make money online. This is where most people go wrong as they just jump and skip to what they see other people do hence opening a straight road to failure. You might make money yes, but for a short while because a business done through copy and paste has no foundation whatsoever.

If you have primary skills, you can match your skills to opportunities like content creation, building print on demand businesses, selling done for you courses or ebooks and so much more.

With secondary skills you can do various admin work, transcription, conducting surveys or reviews, blogging, virtual assistance or even customer service jobs.

With professional skills you can get into web development, offer online consulting sessions, graphic design, marketing, etc.

Keep in mind that you can always work on your skills and upscale to diversify your income streams. It is also important to engage with other people that are in the niche that you are interested in, so as to learn more about new opportunities and trends. You can always get them from the comment section of your favorite social media creators and approach them. They know something you don't or vice versa and which leads to you helping each other. Don't be shy to make the first move.

IDENTIFY YOUR NICHE

Prior to starting any business, you need to know the product that you will sell. The same applies to this. Before getting into any form of online passive income, you need to identify your niche.

Niche is a word that originates from French, specifically from the Middle French verb 'nicher' which means to make a nest. This is a position or activity that suits somebody's talents or personality.

Some of the different niches that exist are:
- Tourism and Travel
- Health and wellness
- Wealth
- Fitness
- Beauty and cosmetics
- Fashion and style
- Lifestyle
- Child care and family life
- Entrepreneurship and Business
- Technology
- Pets
- Music
- Photography

There are several websites and tools that can help you stay updated on trending niches.
These include Google trends that provides insights into what people are searching for over time, wordstream and

Answerthepublic that will help you confirm if your niche is trending.
Trending niches tend to have 30,000 searches or more.
BuzzSumo will help to find popular content within your niche.
It is advised to have a niche that is flexible.
You can combine different niches like fitness and nutrition or others. Keep brainstorming and have an open mind.

Pick a niche that you have interest in and is still profitable. Use the right tools and keep exploring to stay updated on trends and always be ready to adapt to changes.

SETTING UP YOUR ONLINE PRESENCE

To have an online passive income, you need to have a strong online presence to reach out and engage with your audience.

This begins by defining your brand. You need to have a logo, name and bio description. Use SEO keywords to gain organic traffic on your online platform.
Use tools like Google Keyword planner, SEMrush, Ahrefs to find popular search terms related to your interest. These words should be your keywords that will help you optimize the seo search. Consistency is key. Plan and schedule your posts to maintain regular posting. Use tools like Buffer, Hootsuite or Later to manage your social media accounts.

Utilize Email marketing as it is a powerful way to nurture relationships with your audience. Offer valuable incentives like ebooks, free guides or exclusive content to encourage sign up. Send regular newsletters with updates, insights and offers

to the email addresses that you receive. Make sure to personalize them to increase engagement.
Use platforms like flodesk, beacons or mailchimp to manage your email campaigns.

Always analyze your performances to keep track of what content performs and what doesn't. This will help you know what your audience prefers. Use tools like Google analytics or social media insights to monitor your performance. Adjust your approach based on your analysis.

MONETIZING YOUR PLATFORM

This is what transforms your passion into a sustainable source of income. If you have read all the 35 ways to make money online, I assume that you have already set up your mind on the path that you will take on this journey.
This section will explore various monetization strategies and provide practical tips on how to implement them.

- Advertising

This is the most common way to monetize an online platform. The several forms on advertising include :
Display Ads - Platforms like Google Adsense allow you to display ads on your website. You earn money based on clicks or impressions.
Affiliate Marketing - Promote products or services through affiliate links which make you earn commission for each sale made. Some of the popular affiliate programs include Amazon Associates, ShareAsale and Commission Junction.
Sponsored Brands Partnership - Collaborate with brands to create content that promotes their products or services.

- Selling Products or Services.

This is another effective way to monetize your platform. You can do so by selling:

Digital Products - Digital Products barely need any starting capital and high profit margins. Creating and selling ebooks, online courses, printables or software.

Physical Products - Platforms like shopify and etsy make it easy to set up an online store. Sell merchandise related to your brand such as fashion apparel, accessories, jewelleries or custom made items. You can also sell print on demand products which do not really need you to invest money upfront.

- Others.

Refer to 35 sections to learn more of all the other ways.

Integrate your payments with platforms like Payoneer, Paypal, Stripe or others who handle your invoices and payments.

LEGAL CONSIDERATION

As you begin to monetize your online platform, it's crucial to be aware of the legal considerations that can impact your business. It is advised to understand and comply with relevant laws and regulations to avoid any legal issues and maintain trust with your audience.

- **Intellectual Property Rights -** Protecting and respecting other people's IP is fundamental (intellectual property). To do so you have to ensure that all your content is original or properly licensed. Avoid using copyrighted material without permission. If you have a unique product, think of applying for a patent to protect your invention.

- **Privacy and Data Protection -** This is not only a legal requirement but also essential for maintaining trust with your audience. Consider drafting a clear privacy policy that outlines how you collect, use and protect personal data. Make it accessible on your website.

- **Terms of service -** It is important to clearly define terms under which users can interact with your platform. These terms and conditions can cover disclaimers, content ownership, return policy and limitations of liability.

- **E-Commerce Regulations -** If you are selling products or offering services in your niche, ensure that you comply with the e-commerce laws. Provide clear and accurate information about your products and services. Implement secure and compliant payment processing systems. You should be aware of regulations such as the Payment Card Industry Data Security Standard. (PCI DSS)

- **Tax Obligations** - Fulfilling your tax obligations is essential for any type of business or monetized platform. You can consult a tax professional to ensure compliance. Report all generated income from your online activities and pay any applicable income taxes.

CONCLUSION

As you reach the end of this book, you have discovered about the 35 proven ways to make money online. Each method offers unique opportunities, challenges and rewards.

Whether you are looking for an extra income, a replacement for your job, or building a thriving online business, you will definitely find a strategy that can align with your interests, personality, skills and goals.

The power to success is in persistence. All successful people achieved their goals not through simply having an idea but by implementing it and staying consistent.

Remember, success in the online world often requires patience. You might not see immediate rewards, but with consistent effort and willingness to learn and adapt, it is possible to achieve financial goals.

There will always be new platforms that emerge, changes in algorithms and consumer preferences shift. Commit to continuous learning to stay ahead.

The more you learn, the better equipped you'll be to navigate challenges and seize new opportunities.

Diversify your efforts to mitigate risks and create a balanced portfolio of income sources. This will not only enhance your financial stability but also provide a safety net in case one stream faces disruptions.

Finally, remember that your journey is unique. What works for one person might not work for another, and that's okay. Celebrate your success, no matter how small, and learn from your setbacks.

Embrace your journey, stay motivated, and take action. Your path to financial independence is always within reach.

GOODLUCK!!

www.ingramcontent.com/pod-product-compliance
Lightning Source LLC
Chambersburg PA
CBHW071838210526
45479CB00001B/197